Praise for *Blessing and Beseeching*

Dr. Ramshaw brings (as she always has) the melding of an insightful theologian and a sublime poet to this collection of scriptural prayers. These prayers sing, always faithful to the long and living stream of the Judeo-Christian tradition. They are a treasure, for personal or community use.

—Marty Haugen, liturgical composer

Poetic, prophetic, and profoundly prayerful, Gail Ramshaw invites us to be bathed in blessing and to receive balm in our beseeching. Journeying through Scripture, we find our places amidst the petitions of our past for the needs of our own day. If ever there was a need to receive a blessing and to beseech, it is for such a time as this.

—Kevin L. Strickland, bishop, Southeastern Synod of the ELCA

Through her collection of devotional prayers, Gail Ramshaw invites us to call upon the triune God with wonder, curiosity, and bold honesty. Beginning with the Scriptures and her individual experience, these prayers spiral outward to the world's need—needs we may not have thought to name. Ramshaw's wrestling with the Scriptures bestows on the pray-er a rich blessing indeed!

—Jennifer Baker-Trinity, program manager for
Worship Resource Development, ELCA/1517 Media

Your nightstand longs for Ramshaw's treasury of psalm-like prayers evoked by Scriptures from Genesis to Revelation, because there is no richer way to drift into sleep or to awake in the morn than immersed in these pensive, plainspoken conversations with your Creator.

—Peter Bower, editor in chief, *Studia Liturgica*

GW00645289

Gail Ramshaw's influence on liturgy has been remarkable. Her prayers for public worship are found not only in books of her own Evangelical Lutheran Church in America but also in the liturgical resources of Anglican, Methodist, Presbyterian, and United Churches, amongst others. Some of us have struggled to remain in church in hope of the possibilities of renewal which her work proposes. Some of us have sensed in the sound of her prayers the 'aftershocks of the resurrection' for which we yearn in common worship.

Now, in *Blessing and Beseeching*, Gail Ramshaw invites readers to pray her prayers 'for personal use,' as if being invited into her home, to sit at her table or in a room adorned with her beloved Tree of Life—the image with which this book, like the book of Revelation, ends.

Soaked in Scripture throughout, and deeply traditioned, these prayers are full of surprises. Some are disarmingly personal, both open-hearted and straight-talking. Others offer complements—or correctives—to biblical voices, putting forward alternative perspectives: for example, calling for the 'suppression' of a verse in 1 Timothy that would silence women, or enlarging Galatians' list of fruit of the Spirit to put alongside those on 'interior virtues' some on 'outward activism.' Always, the prayers reflect the wideness of God's mercy for the whole world, and in striking ways Ramshaw holds in sight human suffering, keeps the grace of difference in her gaze, and dares some courageous requests, such as that God would 'punch holes' in human-made walls that separate persons from one another.

These prayers are strong, loving, and wise. They are much to be commended between Sundays.

—Stephen Burns, professor of liturgical and pastoral theology,
Pilgrim Theological College, University of Divinity, Melbourne, Australia

Blessing and Beseeching

Blessing and Beseeching

Seventy Prayers Inspired by the Scriptures

GAIL RAMSHAW

FORTRESS PRESS

MINNEAPOLIS

BLESSING AND BESEECHING
Seventy Prayers Inspired by the Scriptures

The Scripture quotation from Judges is from New Revised Standard Version Updated Edition, copyright © 2022.

The Scripture quotation from Isaiah is from *Readings for the Assembly*, cycle B (Minneapolis, MN: Augsburg Fortress, 1996).

All other Scripture quotations are from New Revised Standard Version Bible, copyright © 1989 National Council of the Churches of Christ in the United States of America. Used by permission. All rights reserved worldwide.

Adjustments have been made to Scripture quotations throughout for clarity, brevity, and inclusivity.

Cover image: Daniel Nevins c/o Theispot
Cover design: Laurie Ingram

Print ISBN: 978-1-5064-8499-0
eBook ISBN: 978-1-5064-8500-3

to Esme
Corwin
Ursula
Annika
Kierthan

Contents

Contents

To Begin

Since 1965 I have composed many prayers for use in public worship, but this collection is not intended for the liturgy. During the 2020–21 pandemic, I read once again through the Bible, and I discovered, as the image on the cover of this book suggests, that the Scriptures filled my firmament with vivid, compelling depictions of God, the church, the world, and the self, all of them breaking through the miasma of human need that surrounds us; and mindful of the voices of both Catherine of Siena and Julian of Norwich—the Trinity, always the Trinity—I crafted seventy prayers for personal use, each prayer inspired by a passage in one of the books of the Bible. Some of these seventy are praises to God, some are thanksgivings, and some are petitions, and perhaps some of them can serve your devotion and encourage your own blessing and beseeching.

O God, Father, Son, and Spirit—
Abba, Servant, and Paraclete—
I do not know how to pray as I ought,
    but I thank you for the Scriptures,
in which you heard Miriam praising your name,
and Hannah giving you thanks,
and Mary calling out, "They have no wine."
So, O God, listen to also these prayers.
O sweet Thesaurus of mercy,
teach us to pray.
Amen.

Genesis

*Again Noah sent out the dove from the ark; and the dove
came back to him in the evening, and there in its beak was
a freshly plucked olive leaf. . . . God said, "I have set my
bow in the clouds, and it shall be a sign of the covenant
between me and the earth." Genesis 8:10-11; 9:13*

Thanking God for Baptism

O God, you are the ethereal Rainbow, the
   rough-hewn Ark, the peaceful Dove.
You signal salvation from the flood,
and not only for Noah and the animals,
but in Baptism for all your people, including for me.
I praise you, that on that day long ago,
your multicolor light shimmered in the font,
and your nave was crowded with Sunday worshipers,
as, finished at the Jordan,
you flew all the way to New York City
to hover near my godmother
and offer an olive leaf for my future.
I praise you, O triune God,
for your covenant of Baptism.
Amen.

Exodus

The bush was blazing, yet it was not consumed. Exodus 3:2

PRAISING GOD THE BURNING BUSH

O God, incongruous Fire, inscrutable Paradox,
everything we say about you requires its opposite:
you are aflame, yet nothing is consumed;
you are triune, yet you are one;
you are called Father, yet you are not male;
you demand justice, yet are forever forgiving;
you save us with a mighty hand and an outstretched
     arm, with neither a hand nor an arm;
you are the human Son, yet you created the universe;
you died by execution, yet a god is immortal;
you offer us bread, and we eat your body;
we consume your body, but we are your body;
you are Spirit, beyond the cosmos, yet inside each leaf,
blowing where you will, yet abiding within me.
No wonder the mystics resort to silence.
But not me: I praise you with impossible words,
mind-bending sentences,
proceeding through speech into faith.
Amen.

Leviticus

You are to distinguish between the holy and the common,
and between the unclean and the clean. Leviticus 10:10

Interceding for religious discernment

O God, Sage and Mentor and Visionary, we thought that the purpose of religion is to clarify how to consecrate what, which foods to eat, what gender is, how to keep the self wholly clean inside and out, constantly to separate out the good from the bad. Guided by such regulations, O God, we might know how to live, choosing the holy away from the common. In so doing, the power of evil would not infect or overwhelm the vulnerability of virtue: we would be safe.

Yet in Christianity, O triune God, you have said that nothing is unclean. The holy is found in the common, the almighty lying in a manger, divinity executed, the power of life celebrated by slaves. The sacred is hidden in the profane, God in a mouthful of bread. So how do I know how to live? From which group of Christians can I receive trustworthy advice? Where do we construct a fence, saying, "This far shall you come, and no farther"? Have I any surety about how to distinguish the holy from the common?

O God, give to your people your definition of what is clean and what is unclean. Teach me to honor what is common, and point us toward what radiates with your holiness. And then, in mercy, forgive. Amen.

Numbers

The LORD sent poisonous serpents among the people so that many Israelites died. . . . So Moses made a serpent of bronze, and put it upon a pole; and whenever a serpent bit someone, that person would look at the serpent of bronze and live. Numbers 21:6, 9

INTERCEDING FOR OTHER RELIGIONS

O God of the Hebrew Scriptures, when the Israelites lamented death by snakebite, you appropriated a Canaanite religious symbol to invite your people to repentance. The narrative hides the truth that in the wilderness the goddess Asherah reigning from her tree pole could carry your life to the dying.

Now, O God of all humanity, I pray: continue to reveal yourself through one religion after another. Manifest your mercy, not only through Christ on Calvary, but also through Moses on Sinai; and the Buddha under his bodhi tree; and the black stone of the Kaaba; and the Hindu Trinity of Brahma, Vishnu, and Shiva; and the kami in the sakaki tree; and the sun at the Lakota solstice dance. All we small humans are hoping to connect with the divine, trying one thing or another. Give to us all your blessing. Amen.

Deuteronomy

The Rock . . . is not he your father, who created you? . . .
You were unmindful of the Rock that bore you;
*   you forgot the God who gave you birth. . . .*
Indeed their rock is not like our Rock. Deuteronomy 32:4-6, 18, 31

PRAISING GOD THE ROCK

This ancient poem, O triune God, praises you
    as a male—a father who established us
as an animal—an eagle who guided us
as a female—who bore us and gave us birth
as an it—a fire devouring the earth.
For me, O my God, you have no gender.
We ought not squeeze your mystery into our pronouns.
Yet for a god, perhaps two or three genders are better than one.

On the very edge of a high rock bluff in Maine, with the mossy pathway of the woodlands behind and the salty waves of the ocean far below, I know that to jump is to die by impact, but to stand is to be alive, between a past and a future held in you. Grounded on this created earth, I praise you, O God my Rock. On you I stand. Most rocks are "it," and most deities carved into stone are "he" or "she." But you are beyond such designations: other rocks are not like this Rock. Amen.

Joshua

*About forty thousand armed for war crossed over before the LORD
to the plains of Jericho for battle. . . . Then they devoted to
destruction by the edge of the sword all in the city, both men and
women, young and old, oxen, sheep, and donkeys. Joshua 4:13; 6:21*

INTERCEDING FOR THE END OF WAR

No, no, O God whom we worship: I believe in you, not in the Bible, and so I can reject both the facts and the spirituality of the Joshua narrative, the fantasy that the Israelite invaders had forty thousand warriors and the depiction of you as Headmost Warmonger of People of Faith. That the sun stood still is a charming legend compared with Joshua's genocide, which, inspiring slaughter in your name, has continued its killing spree through the centuries. Folks can say, not that "the devil made me do it," but that you did.

And so we pray:

O God, Maker of peace, Bringer of harmony, everlasting Olive Branch,
bring an end to armed conflicts between and within nations.
Teach forbearance and compromise.
Erase from our vocabulary the mindless term "holy war."
Take toy guns away from children.
Inspire entertainment that does not glorify battle.
Thwart neighborhood gun violence.
Halt genocide.
Give us your peace that passes understanding.
May it be so.

Judges

*At that time Deborah, a prophet, wife of Lappidoth, was judging
Israel. She used to sit under the palm of Deborah between
Ramah and Bethel in the hill country of Ephraim; and the
Israelites came up to her for judgment. Judges 4:4-5*

Interceding for judges

God, you are Chief Justice, Arbiter, and Counselor for your people.
Make of each of us, when called to the task, a worthy Deborah,
ensconced under one of your palm trees,
our limited judgments shaped by your omniscient wisdom.
Direct with your Spirit all the justices and judges in our land.
Give to each a passion for justice,
the insight to distinguish truth from falsehood,
the foresight to sense the future,
the courage to assert what is right,
and the authority to propose just actions for ourselves and others,
through Christ, who is Deborah over all things.
Amen.

Ruth

In the days when the judges ruled, there was a famine in the land . . .
So Ruth gleaned in the field behind the reapers. Ruth 1:1; 2:3

INTERCEDING FOR THE HUNGRY

I lament, O God, Provider, Cornucopia, Life-Giver,
that there are famines,
that women must bow down to gather leftover grain,
that warfare and storms and droughts and wildfires destroy crops,
that migrants must leave their homes to find food,
that starvation maims and kills.
I am sorry, O God, that Naomi tells Ruth to entice
    a benefactor on the threshing floor,
for only in legends are beggar-women rewarded
     by marriage and a royal great-grandson.
I pray to you, O God, for those suffering today from hunger,
children needing free lunches in American schools,
neighbors relying on food pantries,
women buying their bread with their bodies,
refugees reaching out for meager rations.
Feed the hungry, O God.
Equip relief agencies for their food distribution.
Train us to eat less so that others can eat enough.
Fill the earth with your magnanimity.
May it be so.

1 Samuel

Samuel said to Jesse, "Are all your sons here?" And he said, "There remains yet the youngest, but he is keeping the sheep." The LORD said, "Rise and anoint him; for this is the one." 1 Samuel 16:11-12

INTERCEDING FOR SOCIAL CONSERVATIVES

O God, Conservator of the past, Companion in
    the present, Signpost toward the future,
we see that throughout the ages you change the rules,
blessing what had been condemned, rejecting what had been upheld.
Some believers cannot catch up,
six older brothers of the shepherd boy David outraged
when your prophet overturned your tradition of primogeniture.
O changeable God, how am I supposed to know my place in line?
I pray now for all social conservatives,
for whom change is unwelcome,
for whom two genders is quite enough,
for whom divorce is permanent disgrace,
    not a growth experience (can it be both?),
for whom the poor ought to work in order to eat,
for whom obedience to the patriarch constitutes rectitude.
Free those who are shackled to the past for fear of the future.
Strengthen the legs of those who dread to walk a new path,
and grant solicitude to those for whom change seems too slow.
May it be so.

2 Samuel

David said, I am distressed for you, my brother Jonathan;
greatly beloved were you to me;
your love to me was wonderful, passing the
love of women. 2 Samuel 1:26

INTERCEDING FOR THE LGBTQIA+ COMMUNITY

O God, you are the Land of Promise,
in which the Davids and Jonathans may live
    together in dignity and peace of mind.
In our neighborhoods and around the globe,
bless those who are free to live out their gender identity
    and all that it entails.
Grant them security by day and by night,
a community of welcome, the loyalty of friends,
and if they desire it,
a partner to embrace and children to nurture.
Encircle their homes, protect their jobs, and guard their health.
Strengthen their hopefulness, and give them joy.
And to those who are not so free, grant a measure of contentment in you.
In all places, turn opposition to courtesy and antipathy to comradeship.
Shine your image through every person,
and so illumine the Garden of Fulfillment with
    the light of your bountiful goodness.
May it be so.

1 Kings

*Now there was a great wind, so strong that it was splitting mountains
and breaking rocks in pieces before the LORD, but the LORD was
not in the wind; and after the wind an earthquake, but the
LORD was not in the earthquake; and after the earthquake
a fire, but the LORD was not in the fire; and after the
fire a sound of sheer silence. 1 Kings 19:11-12*

PRAISING GOD WHO IS SILENCE

O God, who at creation spoke the world into being,
whose treasured words from the cross echo in our minds,
who calls disciples in every language under the sun,
sometimes we cannot hear you;
there is only your absence,
an emptiness like utter silence.
We keep on babbling,
but you remain mute,
your mouth closed, your back turned to our cries.
Yet, O God, your stillness roused Elijah to faith.
From you comes holy Speech,
and from you comes unutterable Silence—
but also in this sound of nothing is your presence.
When all we hear is the silence,
may we still exhale our praise.
Amen.

2 Kings

The king commanded the priest and the king's servant, saying,
"Go, inquire of the LORD for me." . . . Huldah resided in Jerusalem,
where they consulted her. She declared to them, "Thus says
the LORD, the God of Israel." 2 Kings 22:12-13, 14-15

INTERCEDING FOR WOMEN IN MINISTRY

O God, the Bone and Blood and Breath of your faithful followers, I praise you for the millennia of those women who knew themselves to be your mouthpieces. I laud you for their dedication, their insight, their courage. Some were brash; some were gentle. Some were honored; some were ridiculed. Some in the past were burned as witches; some in the present are ordained.

I thank you for Huldah of Jerusalem, who boldly spoke both law and gospel to the king; for Hilda of Whitby, renowned for her learning, mother abbess of a double monastery of women and men; and for my great aunt Hulda, who a century ago moved away from the prairie to serve as a deaconess in the big bad city.

I ask you to nurture all the Huldahs, those proclaiming your mercy and sharing your energy with their parishioners, those serving as bishops in the many churches, those volunteering for church choirs, those teaching in Sunday schools, those serving on conflicted committees, and those whose ministry is hidden and known only to you. Give to each Huldah in your body an ear to listen to you and a mouth to be your voice. May it be so.

1 Chronicles

*Satan stood up against Israel, and incited David to
count the people of Israel. 1 Chronicles 21:1*

INTERCEDING FOR FORGIVENESS

O God, Lawgiver, Judge, and yet gracious Advocate,
bless me, Father, for I have sinned,
and I will not blame Satan, as did the chronicler, for inciting me.
It is I, in one way or another,
who honored false gods, desecrated your name, criticized worship,
disdained my elders, harmed both neighbors and nature, misused sexuality,
cheated and stolen, lied and slandered,
and coveted what you have given to others.
Out of the mountain of mercy that you have promised us,
forgive, not Satan, but me,
and save me from the pit of myself.
Amen.

2 Chronicles

King Hezekiah stationed the Levites in the house of the LORD with cymbals, harps, and lyres. The whole assembly worshiped, the singers sang, and the trumpeters sounded. They sang praises with gladness. 2 Chronicles 29:25, 28, 30

THANKING GOD FOR HYMN SINGING

O my God, how I love hymns.
Praises to you, O my God, for inventing human song,
for giving us words for our tunes and tunes for our words,
for assembling us into a body of singers.
Receive, O smiling God, our continuous chorus:
two of us concluding breakfast with a hymn;
my family singing by heart at the grave of my mother;
the worshippers laughing at the glissando in "Shine, Jesus, Shine":
a congregation, socially distanced, their faces
    masked, joining in the hymn of the day;
hundreds at a conference chanting, "Jesus, remember me";
a thousand students opening worship with
    "O God, our help in ages past";
and a million of the baptized singing daily at
    prayer, singing weekly at worship,
praising and thanking and interceding
in both sorrow and joy.
O my God, receive my thanks for hymn singing.
Amen.

Ezra

Then Ezra the priest stood up and said to them, "You have trespassed
and married foreign women, and so increased the guilt of Israel.
Now make confession to the LORD the God of your ancestors,
and separate yourselves from the peoples of the land
and from the foreign wives." Ezra 10:10-11

INTERCEDING FOR DISCARDED WOMEN

God, supreme Providence for all humankind,
in Jesus you listened to the cries of women,
and by your Pulse our daughters live.
We lament the many ways that societies discard their women:
female fetuses aborted,
girls undone by sexual abuse,
runaways wrecked by pimps,
women's testimony dismissed,
women's work unpaid—only their sex organs valued,
mothers bled out by repeated pregnancies,
worn-out wives replaced by sweet young things,
tombstones recording only the husband's name.
O God, I ask you to hold in your arms all discarded women;
catch them as they are thrown away,
and give them renewal of life.
Amen.

Nehemiah

The Levites read from the book, from the law of God,
with interpretation. They gave the sense, so that the
people understood the reading. Nehemiah 8:7-8

Interceding for preachers

O God, the Source and the Power of the Logos,
whose scriptures cry out for more clarity, greater illumination,
I praise you for centuries of preachers,
for apostles, bishops, catechists, deacons, evangelists,
for all the priests and pastors who give out the sense of your text,
that the baptized may believe.
I pray for preachers around the globe.
Lead them to proclaim, not themselves, but you.
Give them insight in interpretation,
courage to speak your law,
joy in announcing your gospel—"I have seen the Lord,"
    said Mary Magdalene—
and resilience to continue their task week after week.
Bless, O God, our preachers, this Sunday and next.
Amen.

Esther

*Do not think that in the king's palace you will escape any more
than all the other Jews. Who knows? Perhaps you have come
to royal dignity for just such a time as this. Esther 4:14*

INTERCEDING FOR GOOD GOVERNMENT

O God,
omnipotent Monarch, hidden Messiah, spirited Commonwealth,
Esther's time is also our time:
small-minded heads of state,
autocratic rule,
lavish opulence among civic leaders,
enforced manipulation of women,
murderous advisors,
plans for genocide,
deception in high places,
communal lament.
Give us, beneficent God, good government:
far better than we have,
more virtuous than we deserve,
with a festal banquet at the end.
May it be so.

Job

Can you find out the deep things of God?
Can you find out the limit of the Almighty? Job 11:7

INTERCEDING FOR THEOLOGIANS

O God, you are the Way—too deep to fathom,
the Truth—beyond our limits,
the Life for which we strive.
Like Job, we seek the meaning of your being,
but as with his friends,
our constructs cannot contain the magnitude of human suffering.
Show always more of your depth and distance and mysterious existence
to the theologians of the churches.
Guide their teaching and their writing.
Accompany their study through what is old and what is new.
Grant them stamina when the task is tedious,
humility when a conclusion is reached,
respect for those with whom they disagree,
and always the gratitude of the baptized.
May it be so.

Psalms

The LORD loves the gates of Zion more
*   than all the dwellings of Jacob.*
Glorious things are spoken of you, O city of God.
Singers and dancers alike say, "All my
*   springs are in you." Psalm 87:2-3, 7*

THANKING GOD FOR CITIES

O God, you are our Dwelling Place, you are the Ground beneath our homes.

The psalms say that you love to dwell in Jerusalem, and you promise to gather into that city even historic enemies. And so for Jerusalem I pray that it put away centuries of antagonism and violence and come into a future of stable peace and shared prosperity for peoples of all faiths.

And I pray, O magnanimous God, that you love also New York City, Philadelphia, and Washington D.C. as much as I do. I thank you for giving me a home in these great cities, in which are libraries and art museums; orchestra concerts and dance performances; hospitals and pharmacies; parks to enjoy and a zoo to explore; a choice of churches; and public transportation; and grocery stores with freshly baked bread; and an international airport; and neighbors of every skin color; and ethnic restaurants; and even a seminary or two: all the springs for humanity are here. Praises to you, O God, our City of Hope, for cities, and may your blessings sustain them. Amen.

Proverbs

Wisdom has built her house,
she has mixed her wine, she has also set her table.
She calls from the highest places in the town,
"Come, eat of my bread
and drink of the wine I have mixed.
Lay aside immaturity, and live,
and walk in the way of insight." Proverbs 9:1-3, 5-6

THANKING GOD FOR HOLY COMMUNION

O Christ, Arm of divinity,
first in creation,
Wisdom Woman ordering the cosmos,
Christa in the heavens,
She-Who-Is,
goddess face of the One,
I praise you for hosting the meal of insight.
Glory to you for setting your table with bread and wine.
Feed us with the grain of growth and the juice of joy
that we may mature into the stature you intend,
countless guests in your one mansion,
here for the life of the world.
Amen.

Ecclesiastes

For everything there is a season, and a time for every matter
under heaven: a time to be born, and a time to die . . .
a time to keep, and a time to throw away. Ecclesiastes 3:1-2, 6

INTERCEDING FOR A TIMELY DEATH

O God, as the famous prayer has it,
"Give me work, till my life shall end, and life, till my work is done."
But clean water and healthy food and medical care
    give us life beyond our work,
beyond our usefulness to the earth, to neighbor, to family,
beyond a reliable brain.
O God of merciful edges, O God of a one-day
    dying, O God of flight into the end,
grant to me and to countless others a timely death.
Let me know when that time has come.
Give me contentment with mortality,
earth to earth, ashes to ashes, dust to dust,
you who alone are immortal, you who alone are limitless.
Make me thankful for each breath you have given
until I hand that spirit back to you,
until I bequeath your beneficence to others who need it,
until what remains of me rests in the body of Christ.
Grant me an opportune peace at the last.
Amen.

Song of Solomon

I am my beloved's and my beloved is mine. Song of Solomon 6:3

THANKING GOD FOR SPOUSES

Cavorting intimately under the trees is all very well,
O God, who is Lover, Beloved, and Love itself,
but I thank you for the marriage of aging spouses,
for the daily rituals of sharing place and time,
for seeing one another across the table,
for walking side by side on ordinary adventures,
for nights held together despite all the darknesses,
for prayers spoken together as one.
I do know of vows that were broken;
but for each treasured commitment that stood firm
—a castle cemented over the decades,
a tent still standing despite tempests—
through parallel pains and grace-filled joys,
for the love that was shaken together and running over
and thus served out to others near and far,
I thank you.
Amen.

Isaiah

One seraph called to another and said: "Holy,
    holy, holy is the LORD of hosts;
the whole earth is full of the glory of the LORD." Isaiah 6:3

THANKING GOD FOR THE EARTH

O Three-in-One God, I glimpse the seraphs burning with adoration,
and I join their chant of "Holy, holy, holy"—
the Father incomprehensible, the Son incomprehensible,
    the Spirit incomprehensible—
praising you for a whole earth that is full of your glory.
For four billion years you oversaw the formation of a providential earth
with its flawless food chain nurturing creatures known and unknown.
I thank you for a double rainbow, and purple fields of heather,
and Monument Valley, and the bluffs on the Maine coast,
and nurse logs in the rain forests,
and a leafy sea dragon, and sea otters,
and migrating monarch butterflies blanketing a tree,
and corn on the cob with a tad of butter and a touch of salt,
and each unique opal.
Yes, the whole earth is full of you: better than a heaven.
Thank you, Jesus, King of creation.
Amen.

Jeremiah

*Just like the clay in the potter's hand, so are you in
my hand, O house of Israel. Jeremiah 18:6*

PRAISING GOD THE POTTER

We praise you, O God, we acclaim you as Potter:
a patient and precise artist,
you prepare the clay, you model perfect form, you delight in design.
Your labor in shaping your human creations is endless:
yesterday repairing a crack, today refluting the rim,
    tomorrow adding a touch of new color,
never in righteous exasperation smashing us to bits.
Make me content to be the vessel that you have formed.
Mold us all for your purposes,
that we may embody your creativity
and manifest your mastery,
to the glory of your consummate name.
Amen.

Lamentations

My eyes flow with rivers of tears because of the
destruction of my people. Lamentations 3:48

Interceding for relief during epidemics

I remember before you, O God, times of plague:
locusts in Judah, bubonic death in Europe,
smallpox and measles among aborigines,
Spanish flu and yellow fever and Covid around the globe—
invisible armies laying waste to one population after another.
God our Refuge, preserve humankind from devastation.
God our Physician, heal the sick.
God our Nurse, sustain the caregivers.
God our Friend, accompany the fearful.
God our Comforter, console the bereaved.
God our Mother, embrace the dying.
God our Shield, protect the vulnerable.
God our Tent, shelter the homeless.
God our Governor, deliver food and water.
O triune God, give us some blessing:
God our Creator, renew our world.
God our Savior, rescue the sufferers.
God our Guardian, restore safety to society.
O triune God, rectify all things. Amen.

Ezekiel

As I was among the exiles by the river Chebar, the heavens
were opened, and I saw visions of God. Ezekiel 1:1

THANKING GOD FOR VISIONARIES

O God, Mystery beyond knowing, invisible
    Salvation, transcendent Holiness,
I offer my gratitude for those believers who, viewing a cloud,
glimpse not water vapor but your ineffable majesty.
I laud you for those who have seen what others do not see.
When the cosmos has been upended, and the heavens are opened,
through the rift these visionaries perceive, oh,
four many-eyed creatures on a wheel within a wheel;
or innumerable choirs of angels;
or two men in dazzling clothes;
or the horse-rider with a sword extending from his mouth;
or twelve gates opening to a radiant city, clear as crystal;
or a dragon's head become a stepstool;
or a white-haired shepherd serving a mouthful of milk;
or the blazing branches on the pillar of the word of God;
or a wedding ring, engraved, received, and worn.
I thank you for these visions, not mine to experience,
but rather to ponder in mute pleasure.
Amen.

Daniel

This is a public decree: if you do not tell me both the dream and its interpretation, you shall be torn limb from limb, and your houses shall be laid in ruins. . . . Therefore I make a decree: Any people, nation, or language that utters blasphemy against the God of Shadrach, Meshach, and Abednego shall be torn limb from limb, and their houses laid in ruins. Daniel 2:5, 3:29

INTERCEDING FOR THE DEFEAT OF DICTATORS

O God, I grin as King Nebuchadnezzar bellows, threatening destruction and death, for this is only a story. But Hitler, Stalin, Mao, Mussolini, Pinochet, Franco, Amin, and their gang are the horrific facts of human history, and toddler despots are climbing out of their playpens, awaiting their turn as oppressors.

O God, benevolent Majesty, sovereign Champion, Realm of justice, thwart—no, prohibit—the reign of tyrants.

Mute their rhetoric, and expose their lies.

Quell the power of their charism, and blunt the rage that supports them.

Stand with the military that stands against the autocrats.

Strengthen democracies, and encourage the vote.

Bolster the resolve of elected legislators and appointed judges.

Emend established law, that grievances may be lessened.

Give each nation a sense of its rightful place in a crowded world.

Reveal your dominion to the weak and to the powerful,

and may all persons live in peace and with honor.

May it be so.

Hosea

When I fed them, they were satisfied;
they were satisfied, and their heart was proud;
therefore they forgot me. . . .
I will fall upon them like a bear robbed of her cubs,
and will tear open the covering of their heart. Hosea 13:6, 8

PRAISING GOD THE MOTHER BEAR

O God, wild Bear,
mutilating any who would harm your cubs,
unrestrained in protecting your offspring,
ferocious against enemies,
the church is hesitant to stand before your
    brutal force—do you still have it?—
or is your mothering now only gentle,
tender-hearted when peril approaches?
O untamable God,
sometimes I wish for your violence,
your tearing apart evil into tiny powerless pieces.
Meanwhile I praise you,
as, careful of your claws,
you direct us into your dark den of safety.
Amen.

Joel

The fields are devastated, the ground mourns;
for the grain is destroyed, the wine dries up, the oil fails. . . .
The vine withers, the fig tree droops.
Pomegranate, palm, and apple–all the
    trees of the field are dried up;
surely, joy withers away among the people. Joel 1:10, 12

INTERCEDING FOR THE DESPOILED EARTH

O God, our Sun, our Morning Star, our Rain and Wind,
our carelessness and selfishness have marred the
    unutterable beauty of your earth,
trashing your forests and polluting your air,
replacing your heavenly supervision with our irresponsible ways.
The old prayers, O God, named you almighty and merciful—
and so I beg you: be once again almighty and merciful.
Cleanse the seas, purify the rivers, protect the shorelines,
lower earth's temperatures, preserve the ice sheets, send more snow,
provide rain in drought, lessen hurricane force,
halt wildfires, remove smog,
restore plant life, maintain habitats for all your creatures.
Inhibit the calamities that humans have engendered,
empower our resolve to save your creation,
and renew the spirits of those of us who remain.
Amen.

Amos

I hate, I despise your festivals,
and I take no delight in your solemn assemblies. . . .
Take away from me the noise of your songs;
I will not listen to the melody of your harps. Amos 5:21, 23

INTERCEDING FOR ACCEPTABLE WORSHIP

These are harsh words, O God,
our Temple, our Chalice, divine Presence among us,
especially for those of us who love the liturgy.
Is our worship indeed so meager, or our level of
    righteousness so low, that you cannot bear it?
During the coronavirus, good God, you had your
    way, hearing only the silence of the stars,
for we prayed softly in our homes, laying aside
    our harps, cowering from infection.
But now, O God, week by week, year by year,
be our redoubtable Ringmaster,
and order our festivals and conduct our assemblies,
    to your delight and our need,
accepting our worship in your everlasting forbearance.
Amen.

Obadiah

But you should not have gloated over your
brother on the day of his misfortune;
you should not have boasted on the day of distress. Obadiah 12

INTERCEDING FOR EMPATHY

O God, Master of the palace, Mistress of the manor,
    Overseer of the universe,
I am only an obadiah, a servant in your kingdom.
But I want always to be more,
and so I strut when others fall down,
I brag when others are laid low.
As if life were a board game, and my friend must lose so that I can win,
save me, O God, from schadenfreude.
As if I am competing in the Olympics,
stop me, O God, from preening when I am half of one second ahead.
Give me only suitable pride, and genuine gratitude,
and always ready sympathy toward others.
May it be so.

Jonah

The LORD provided a large fish to swallow up Jonah; and Jonah was in the belly of the fish three days and three nights. Jonah 1:17

INTERCEDING FOR SAFETY AT SEA

Jesus Christ, God's Son, Savior,
I never learned how to swim,
and so, O Ichthys,
when the breakers are overwhelming,
when my boat is sinking down, sinking down,
when I go overboard,
hear my gasping prayer:
be there for me,
as you were for defiant Jonah.
O you unfathomable Fish,
swallow me up and carry me to safety.
And always, every day,
ferry to safe harbor all those who are fishing for their day's catch,
and rescue all the boat people who are falling off their rafts.
Deliver them all to dry land.
May it be so.

Micah

O my people, what have I done to you?
In what have I wearied you? Answer me! Micah 6:3

THANKING GOD FOR OUR JEWISH ROOTS

Listening to Micah condemn the people's behavior,
my memory returns me to church on Good Friday,
hearing you, O God, reproach our faithlessness,
to which we reply:
Holy God, holy and mighty, holy and immortal, have mercy on us.
Especially on our High Holy Days I thank you
    for our ancestral Judaism—
as we borrow their Hosannas on Palm Sunday,
and remember Passover on Maundy Thursday,
and beg forgiveness on Good Friday,
and dance on the safe side of the sea at the Vigil,
and enjoy manna on Easter Day,
and sing Alleluia for the next forty days.
Give to us Christians gratefulness for our Hebrew roots
and respect for the Jewish tree that grows next to our own.
Holy God, holy and mighty, holy and immortal, we glorify your name.
Amen.

Nahum

Devastation, desolation, and destruction!
Hearts faint and knees tremble,
all loins quake, all faces grow pale!
See, I am against you, says the LORD of hosts, and I
*   will burn your chariots in smoke. Nahum 2:10, 13*

PRAISING GOD THE EARTHQUAKE

The prophet said that your fury, O God, is global chaos redux,
that your anger can destroy the beauteous order of Genesis,
that your wrath at our conduct is earthquake and volcano, fire and storm.
Yet I will praise you, righteous God, even if and while you rage,
for your promise, gracious God, of a salutary landscape,
a terrain renewed in grace.
But what about the rage of the oppressed,
who roar with wrath against injustice,
who smolder under a society built on their backs?
O God, the inexplicable Earthquake,
gather their justifiable anger into your creative force,
that all people will praise you,
as perhaps without tumult
you renew the face of the earth.
Amen.

Habakkuk

Though the fig tree does not blossom, and no fruit is on the vines;
though the produce of the olive fails, and the fields yield no food;
though the flock is cut off from the fold, and
  there is no herd in the stalls,
yet I will rejoice in the LORD; I will exult in the
  God of my salvation. Habakkuk 3:17-18

Interceding for a Habit of Gratitude

O God, everlasting Giver, perpetual Gift, overflowing Treasure Chest,
form me into a habit of gratitude,
so that I arise every morning praising you,
so that at every meal I bless you,
so that waiting in line for my turn, I hum a gloria,
so that I fall asleep each night thanking you.
May it be you whom I am grateful for,
rather than merely for all the good things I receive from you,
or for some salvation other than yourself that I might achieve.
For better for worse, for richer for poorer, in sickness and in health,
I thank you.
May it be so.

Zephaniah

*At that time I will change the speech of the
peoples to a pure speech. Zephaniah 3:9*

Interceding for Pure Speech

O God, Author of luminous language, Speaker
   of truth, Inspiration for our discourse,
whatever pure speech is, I want it.
From my mouth no more cheap slang, no more sarcasm,
nothing vulgar, nothing obscene:
give me speech clearer than clean water,
honest, unsullied, heartfelt,
eloquent, in place of arrogant,
utterances worthy of a creature created for the word.
Remove from my mind those hurtful judgments
that jump out when I am careless,
and replace plain nastiness with simple courtesy.
May it be so.

Haggai

*On that day, says the LORD of hosts, I will take you
and make you like a signet ring; for I have chosen
you, says the LORD of hosts. Haggai 2:23*

THANKING GOD FOR ROYAL APPROVAL

Everlasting Crown, merciful Regent, shared Potentate,
I thank you for every sign of your royal favor, and I delight in
    your fantastic promise to grant me a signet ring. It might be
    engraved with a Chi-Rho for all the world to see. But perhaps
    you have countless such rings, innumerable signs of your infinite
    sovereign approval, presented to those you have chosen.
Perhaps the rings of the Orthodox show the three at Mamre's meal,
Lutherans select the cross,
Roman Catholics are delighted with their Mary,
evangelicals their open book;
fierce preachers don the sign of the sword of the word,
church musicians David's lyre,
green Christians your sun and moon.
I thank you for choosing also me to boast a ring of your power.
I'll be glad of a tree-of-life on mine,
along with guidance on when to employ your seal of authority,
this imaginative golden gift of divine approval.
Amen.

Zechariah

Jerusalem shall be inhabited like villages without walls.
For I will be a wall of fire all around it, says the LORD,
and I will be the glory within it. Zechariah 2:4-5

PRAISING GOD THE WALL OF FIRE

You promised, O God,
that you would encircle your people with protective fire,
so that the glory of your presence would prohibit evil any entry,
your mysterious flames keeping us safe from assault.
Yet both beyond your wall, in distant fields,
and within our homes, our churches, our cities, our lands,
we see disease and distrust, hate and hunger, poverty and perversity.
And we know in terror about uncontrollable walls of fire,
signaling an altered earth,
destroying communities, ravaging forests,
    burning firefighters beyond repair.
I beg you, O Fiery Barrier, to be our only flaming wall,
an incongruous firebreak that saves us,
inside and out, now and forever.
Amen.

Malachi

But for you who revere my name the sun of righteousness
shall rise, with healing in its wings. Malachi 4:2

Interceding for healing

O God, are you a shaman with a drum?
a neurosurgeon with microinstruments?
Isis, forever reanimating her dead brother?
I probe your promise that you will heal:
Must we first revere your name?
Does our wholeness come naturally from the rising sun?
How is the sun righteous?
Does health fly towards us, on unseen wind?
However your healing comes,
Healer, Wounded One, Consoler,
send it now, I pray—
to diseased bodies and disordered minds,
to those awaiting a dreaded diagnosis and those
    who can never visit a physician,
to infants born blind and lame toddlers and addicted teenagers,
to that lady down the block with lifelong pain—
heal us, we pray.
Amen.

Tobit, from the Apocrypha

The young man went out and the angel went with him. Tobit 6:1

INTERCEDING FOR TRAVELERS

O God, you are our Protector, our Guardian Angel, our Compass.
I pray that you travel with us, wherever we go.
Accompany the children walking to school,
the teenagers jammed into a car,
families riding on buses,
adults flying here and there for business or vacation,
relatives gathering for festivals,
the aged driven to the emergency ward.
Join us on our bikes and motorcycles, our cars and taxicabs,
our trains and planes, even on our ferries and cruise ships.
Keep from us harm and danger.
And I beg that you safeguard also those journeys of desperation,
the refugees fleeing violence,
the migrants searching for jobs,
the minorities escaping genocide.
Grant that they may arrive at their destination
in health, in safety, and in joy.
Amen.

Wisdom of Solomon, from the Apocrypha

Wisdom is radiant and unfading,
and she is easily discerned by those who love her,
and is found by those who seek her. Wisdom 6:12

INTERCEDING FOR WISDOM

O God, Origin of knowledge, itinerant Teacher,
   omniscient Enlightenment,
we search for wisdom,
which, despite what this compelling poem claims, is not easily found.
We look in many places:
shelved in libraries, hanging in art museums,
enjoyed in zoos, discovered in science labs,
buried underground, told by our grandmothers,
encountered during prayer, preached by our pastors,
heard in music, received through tears,
offered by friends, glimpsed during dreams.
Direct me and all who seek wisdom to where it might be granted,
and surprise me today with some small insight,
a speck of your wisdom,
a gift of at least some understanding.
Amen.

Prayer of Azariah, from the Apocrypha

Blessed are you, O Lord, God of our ancestors,
and to be praised and highly exalted forever. . . .
Let the earth bless the Lord. . . .
Bless the Lord, all that grows in the ground. . . .
Prayer of Azariah 29, 52, 54

THANKING GOD FOR TREES

Bless the Living One, all dogwoods, announcing the coming of spring;
sing praise to God, who is highly exalted forever.
Bless the Living One, all cherry trees, blossoming in Washington;
sing praise to God, who is highly exalted forever.
Bless the Living One, all maples, turning yellow,
    orange, red, and purple in the fall;
sing praise to God, who is highly exalted forever.
Bless the Living One, all fir trees, decorating our homes at Christmas;
sing praise to God, who is highly exalted forever.
Bless the Living one, all paper birch, lightening the woods in Maine;
bless the Living One, all redwoods, towering above the pathways;
bless the Living One, all umbrella pines, delighting the visitors in Rome;
bless the Living One, all monkey puzzle trees, making us laugh;
sing praise to God, who is highly exalted forever.
Bless the Living One, all the trees I have never seen;
sing praise to God, who is highly exalted forever.
Amen.

Susanna, from the Apocrypha

Then Susanna cried out with a loud voice, and said, "O eternal
God, you know what is secret and are aware of all things
before they come to be; you know that these men have
given false evidence against me." Susanna 42-43

INTERCEDING FOR THE CRIMINAL JUSTICE SYSTEM

O God, who is above, within, and around our
    attempts at rectitude in society,
I stand with Susanna to plead for an honorable criminal justice system.
That you will attend to our land with your merciful law, we pray:
that the innocent are not falsely accused;
that police do not resort to violence;
that the accused are treated fairly;
that pretrial arrangements are legal;
that prosecutors and defense attorneys are trustworthy;
that juries are conscientious;
that judges are upright;
that those incarcerated are granted respect;
that prison chaplains are supported;
that prisoners do not harass or harm one another;
that those released from prison find welcome;
that capital punishment be abolished.
In the name of Jesus of Nazareth, who was falsely accused, illegally tried,
cruelly executed, yet vindicated by your Spirit, we pray. Amen.

Matthew

Go therefore and make disciples of all nations, baptizing
them in the name of the Father and of the Son
and of the Holy Spirit. Matthew 28:19

PRAISING THE TRINITY

Three-in-One God, which name best praises you?
Paul taught us Lord Jesus Christ, God, and Holy Spirit;
Tertullian wrote Root, Stem, Fruit; and Ephrem, Sun, Light, Heat.
For Augustine, you are Lover, Beloved, Love, and
    also Memory, Understanding, Will.
Should I join Hildegard with Wine, Bread, Water,
    or Mechthild with Heart, Body, Breath,
or Catherine with Table, Food, Server,
    or Julian with Maker, Lover, Keeper?
Is George Herbert's my Light, my Feast, my Strength better?
Then there's Karl Barth's Veiling, Unveiling, Imparting,
and William Hill's Being, Knowing, Loving,
and Ruth Duck's Mother, Brother, Partner,
and Elizabeth Johnson's Spirit-Sophia, Jesus-Sophia, Mother-Sophia,
and David Cunningham's Source, Wellspring, Living Water. . . .
One-in-three God, I pour the elixir of life into three crystal carafes,
but the stoppers don't quite fit,
and so some of your essence escapes into your air.
Accept my praise, anyway, any way.
Amen.

Mark

With what can we compare the kingdom of God? It is like a mustard
seed, which, when sown upon the ground, is the smallest of all
the seeds on earth; yet when it is sown it grows up and becomes
the greatest of all shrubs, and puts forth large branches, so that
the birds of the air can make nests in its shade. Mark 4:30-32

INTERCEDING FOR IMAGINATION

The scholars tell us, O mythmaker God,
that behind Mark's parable of a mustard bush
is the legend of the archetypal tree of life
in which all the birds of the air will make their nests.
But, O hidden God, your dominion is concealed inside nature,
your merciful kingdom is beyond my fingertips.
All that is before me is a mustard shrub,
just a common plant with a bird or a bug,
a scraggly weed that yields only an optional spice.
Give me, unseen God, your imagination beyond our facts.
Grant me insight into what cannot be known,
certitude that within this bush is your transformative power,
confidence that in the seed is the full harvest,
the faith that in Calvary's tree is fruitful life for all.
May it be so.

Luke

You will conceive in your womb and bear a son,
and you will name him Jesus. Luke 1:31

INTERCEDING FOR HEALTHY PREGNANCIES

O our God, you are the Progenitor of life, the Infant born of a woman,
the Genesis of breath in every human. From Eve on—"I have
produced a man with the help of the LORD"—the stories say that
many women received your help to conceive and bear: Sarah,
Rebekah, Rachel, Hannah, Elizabeth, Mary. For we know that
what is ironically named Mother Nature is not a reliable provider
of successful pregnancy and healthy childbirth. And so I pray:
give pregnancy to those who desire a child;
support them as they labor;
lessen their pain;
console those who cannot conceive;
comfort those who cannot bring offspring to term;
accompany those who rue their pregnancy;
bring to life children who are whole and well;
sustain the mothers and fathers as they raise their young;
and welcome to yourself the women who die in giving birth.
And may it be that many parents join Mary
in treasuring each child
and in rejoicing in you, their Savior.
Amen.

John

*Jesus said to them, "Very truly, I tell you, before Abraham was,
I am." So they picked up stones to throw at him. John 8:58-59*

PRAISING GOD THE I AM

O God, the eternal Existence, enfleshed in Jesus, the son of Joseph from Nazareth, nearly stoned to death for heresy, I praise you, the great I AM.

I have called on your name for praise and petition: give me, O God, more names, to fill up the spaces in your openness. And the fourth evangelist, soaring untamed, flying highest, seeing farthest, does just that: Jesus is the Word, Lamb, Son, Rabbi, Messiah, an Israelite who is King of Israel, Son of Man, temple, bridegroom, water, the prophet, bread, Holy One, light of the world, gatekeeper, gate, good shepherd, the resurrection, teacher, lord, way, truth, life, vine, friend, King of the Jews, all these, my Lord and my God.

Praise to you. Each image recolors the next, each figure of speech slightly altering the direction we are to travel to join one another in your heart. I wonder: how many believers helped the evangelist assemble this list? When one image fails us and we strain to believe, there are dozens more, upholding our flight, calling us to the cross, to all who suffer, to yourself.

Praise to you. Even the cohort of Roman soldiers, busy arresting you in the garden, must pause in their task as they fall to the ground before you.

Amen.

Acts

*The Hellenists complained because their widows were being
neglected in the daily distribution of food. "Select seven men
of good standing full of the Spirit and of wisdom, whom
we may appoint to this task." And they chose Stephen, a
man full of faith and the Holy Spirit. Acts 6:1, 3, 5*

INTERCEDING FOR DIACONAL MINISTERS

On the newly baptized, come, Holy Spirit, wind and flame.
On each assembly of worshippers, come, Holy Spirit, wind and flame.
On all diaconal ministers, come, Holy Spirit, wind and flame.
On the daily ministry the deacons perform,
    come, Holy Spirit, wind and flame.
On their service at the table of the word,
    come, Holy Spirit, wind and flame.
On their service at the tables of the poor,
    come, Holy Spirit, wind and flame.
Blow your creative wind into the air they inhale.
Transport the fire of Sinai onto each deacon's forehead.
Enrich the whole church with their commitment.
Consecrate each deacon with your love: come, Holy Spirit, wind and fire!
May it be so.

Romans

*When we cry, "Abba! Father!" it is that very Spirit bearing witness
with our spirit that we are children of God, and if children, then
heirs, heirs of God and joint heirs with Christ. Romans 8:15-17*

PRAISING ABBA GOD

O incomprehensible, unutterable Holy One,
Paul invites me to call you Abba,
addressing you with a child's cry of love and need and trust.
Grant that I may continue to find surprising grace in such a prayer,
a door wide open to your presence—
even for us adult women—
and a bond with millions of siblings who inhabit your house.
Nurture me through life until death, as a loving parent would.
Rear me to value my status as a beneficiary of your beloved gifts
and an inheritor of your inscrutable trinitarian promises.
So: Abba, Amen.

1 Corinthians

For just as the body is one and has many members,
and all the members of the body, though many, are
one body, so it is with Christ. 1 Corinthians 12:12

INTERCEDING FOR THE BODY OF CHRIST

O Jesus Christ, once in and yet always beyond physicality,
I pray for the well-being of your body:
the body of Christ—each member separate, yet all members together;
the body of Christ—each Sunday assembling,
   so we can become what we are;
the body of Christ—all speaking and singing together, the many as one;
the body of Christ—at the intercessions,
   the whole aching when one is in pain;
the body of Christ—at the passing of the peace,
   my neighbor clasping my arms;
the body of Christ—at the eucharist,
   one small piece of a loaf in my mouth;
the body of Christ—on Maundy Thursday,
   a worshiper's bare foot in my hand;
the body of Christ—every believer in each time zone
   crowded into my mind.
To you, O Jesus Christ, I pray:
hold your body together,
since its parts can too easily fall away from the whole.
Fortify and safeguard your body,
which is strong enough to conquer death
but, when piecemeal, is frail enough to fail.
Amen.

2 Corinthians

*Blessed be the God of all consolation, who consoles us in
all our affliction, so that we may be able to console those
who are in any affliction with the consolation with which
we ourselves are consoled by God. 2 Corinthians 1:3-4*

INTERCEDING FOR PASTORAL COUNSELORS

O God, you listen to our cry of pain,
you embrace us in our need,
you dwell in those who provide consolation.
I thank you for the many who join with you
to carry out your ministry of care.
Give to family, friends, deacons, pastors, therapists, nurses, and physicians
the grace to listen to cries of pain,
the knowledge to comfort those in need,
the patience to embody your consolation.
Grant to all pastoral counselors the insight to know
how to hear, when to hug, whom to solace,
and make all of us willing to hold others in your care.
May it be so.

Galatians

The fruit of the Spirit is love, joy, peace, patience,
kindness, generosity, faithfulness, gentleness,
and self-control. Galatians 5:22-23

INTERCEDING FOR OTHER FRUITS OF THE SPIRIT

O God, Storehouse of all good things, we praise you for nurturing
your people with your Spirit, the spirit of love, joy, peace,
patience, kindness, generosity, faithfulness, gentleness, and
self-control. Give us always more of these fruits, bushel
baskets filled with such bounty. But while you are at it,
lionhearted God, I need also other fruits of your Spirit:
boldness for the truth;
impatience with hypocrisy;
defiance against injustice;
courage to confront evil;
stamina for the struggle;
passion for cooperative service.
Cultivate in your people, not only interior virtue,
but also outward activism,
and grant that I produce a yield
which thwarts what is wrong and advances the welfare of the needy.
May it be so.

Ephesians

*For Christ is our peace; in his flesh he has made both groups
into one and has broken down the dividing wall, that
is, the hostility between us. Ephesians 2:14*

INTERCEDING FOR AN END TO PREJUDICE

O God, you are beyond and within the one globe of the earth,
you are risen above our boundaries,
you bestow peace beyond our understanding.
You invite us to live without hostility,
to demolish dividing walls,
to be the one human race that you love.
But our cribs and playpens have protective bars,
and we are creatures who by nature are walled in with our kind.
The walls of our prejudices are many:
skin color, ethnic origin, sexual identity, religious choice, familial
    language, native diet, political party, preferred holidays,
    employment arena, music preference, bodily gestures—what else?
When is it ever true that "good fences make good neighbors"?
But now I pray:
give us grace to form our many groupings into an outlandish unity.
With your merciful might, O God, punch holes in our walls,
that we see beyond our barriers into your
    multitudinous world and its myriad peoples
and rejoice in your dumbfounding diversity.
May it be so.

Philippians

*Whatever is true, whatever is honorable, whatever is just,
whatever is pure, whatever is pleasing, whatever is commendable,
if there is any excellence and if there is anything worthy
of praise, think about these things. Philippians 4:8*

INTERCEDING FOR EXCELLENCE

In a time when deceit, cynicism, and violence are rampant,
O God of Beauty, Humanity's Holiness, Treasury of Excellence,
I pray for more signs of your perfection in our ungodly world:
for news broadcasts that are true,
government officials who are honorable,
law enforcement that is just,
conversation that is pure,
entertainment that is pleasing,
fiction and film that are commendable,
toward thoughts that are worthy of your praise,
toward communities that reflect your will.
I ask also for religion without irony,
a taste of bread and wine without any bitterness,
shared Sundays transfigured by your excellence.
May it be so.

Colossians

*You have stripped off the old self with its practices
and have clothed yourselves with the new self, which
is being renewed in knowledge according to the
image of its creator. Colossians 3:9-10*

Interceding for the image of God

O God, Creator of humanity, Firstborn of newness, Fullness of divinity, who clothes us with righteousness and renews earth's likeness to the holy, we are told that in ancient times adults were baptized naked, first washing off their old self and then, bearing your image, they donned the white robe of those gathered in the heavenly court.

And so I ask: what is this image of yours that we bear? Does it mean that we rule over the other animals? Or was the serpent correct, that being like you meant knowing good from evil? History offers many other answers: that your image is immortality, relationality, sinlessness, free will, bisexual reciprocity, responsibility for earth care—each answer reflecting the culture in which it arose. Now I am hearing that also cats have your image.

Grant us, O God, your image, whatever it might be. Imprint on us your trinitarian incomprehensibility of the First, the Only, the Whole. Empower us to walk upright, to safeguard animals, to live unafraid of death, to connect in love with one another, to think wisely, to act morally, to enact truthful self-awareness, to find sexuality enhanced, and together to care for creation.

Renew us, O God, in, by, and for your image.

Amen.

1 Thessalonians

We also constantly give thanks to God for this, that when you received the word of God that you heard from us, you accepted it not as a human word but as what it really is, God's word, which is also at work in you believers. 1 Thessalonians 2:13

THANKING GOD FOR THE LECTIONARY

O God who spoke the word, who is the word, who actuates the word,
I praise you for the lectionary, the scriptures we have selected
that sanctify the year,
inaugurate the week,
unite the churches,
guide the preacher,
reveal the Trinity,
proclaim Christ,
bestow grace,
foster resources,
and encourage study.
Your gift of the lectionary provides worshipers with enough
and protects worshipers from too much.
Grant a steadfast faith to all who endorse the lectionary
and to all who receive these readings as your word.
Until next Sunday,
Amen.

2 Thessalonians

*So then, stand firm and hold fast to the traditions
that you were taught by us, either by word of
mouth or by our letter. 2 Thessalonians 2:15*

THANKING GOD FOR TRADITIONS

O God, always ancient, always new,
the Inception and the Summit and the Culmination of all things,
as we humans search for meaning, always for more meaning,
I praise you when our past practices can enhance our present actions.
I thank you that the dark at Christmas is illumined by the winter solstice,
that Easter is set by the movements of earth and moon.
I thank you that candles adorn even our well-lit sanctuaries,
that our Lent is marked by the ashes of our repentant ancestors,
that we sing "A Mighty Fortress" once a year,
and I am glad for a Good Friday menu of noodles and prunes,
my grandmother's piety nourishing my own.
But with my thanks, O God, comes a prayer
that you help us to bury those traditions that are only coffins,
that you show us where to unearth treasures
    that were prematurely interred,
that you uphold us in preserving worthy practices.
So I will thank you for traditions that enrich our joy
    and those that embrace our sorrow,
traditions ancient, traditions new,
each making more of me than I can make of myself.
Amen.

1 Timothy

I permit no woman to teach or to have authority over
a man; she is to keep silent. 1 Timothy 2:12

Interceding for women's voices

O outspoken Savior,
I pray for the suppression of this man's notorious command.
You created us humans with the multiform phenomenon of the voice;
now make room for all these voices to be heard.
As you proclaimed the resurrection
   through the mouth of Mary Magdalene,
now open the mouth of every woman who has been silenced.
Free all persons from the historic pattern of master and slave.
Release all persons from the stereotypes of gendered speech.
Give to all persons voices that are both gentle and assertive,
both authoritative and deferential.
Give a platform to everyone, the binary, the nonbinary,
so that we hear from all the baptized both law and gospel.
Teach every believer to sing the Magnificat,
as loudly and as continuously as possible.
Amen.

2 Timothy

*I am reminded of your sincere faith, a faith that lived first
in your grandmother Lois and your mother Eunice
and now, I am sure, lives in you. 2 Timothy 1:5*

Interceding for grandmothers

For myself and for millions of grandmothers I pray,
O God, the Ancient of Days.
Embrace with your venerable and wrinkled arms all the women
who care for grandchildren, who comfort them in distress,
who serve them food and nurse their wounds,
who purchase them gifts and provide them adventures,
who tell them of the past and read them stories,
who take them to church and sing them a hymn—
those who assist the parents and those who replace the parents,
whether the children carry their genes or hail from other households.
Give to grandmothers wisdom in judgment,
stamina in weariness, resilience after exhaustion,
joy inside any sorrow, freedom from resentment,
and always enough resources for endless multitasking.
Make each grandmother a Lois
through whom your goodness lives on in the children.
May it be so.

Titus

Let people learn to devote themselves to good works in order to meet urgent needs, so that they may not be unproductive. Titus 3:14

INTERCEDING FOR RETIRED PERSONS

O obstreperous God, Titus is very big on obedience: believers to their bishops, wives to their husbands, the youth to the aged, slaves to their masters, subjects to their rulers. Grant me the insight to know which regulations do provide appropriate guidance. On the other hand, give me the mettle to follow believers, saints, visionaries, and martyrs in crossing the lines, with boldness of action and independence of choice, our good works disregarding the specifics of ancient and sterile household codes. Although I am an aged one, tell me when to hearken to the youth.

Yet this one verse at the close of Titus gives me pause: and so I pray for the multitudes of retired persons, myself included, who no longer awaken to an alarm clock, who are past any obedience to the employer. Show us what we are to do with our passions and our energies. Bend our travels toward service. Point me toward urgent needs, that throughout the years—perhaps even decades—of my remaining days, I will be fully productive, devoted to those in need, contributing whatever I can, perhaps generating something new, until my life is done.

May it be so.

Philemon

I am sending Onesimus, that is, my own heart, back to you . . .
that you might have him back forever, no longer as a slave but
more than a slave, a beloved brother. Philemon 12, 15-16

Interceding for the enslaved

We do not know, O God the Liberator,
what happened to Onesimus.
But the sacred stories say that you free the slaves,
that you stand with the shackled.
So I pray now for deliverance for all who are enslaved:
for men walking on the roadside near the prison guards;
for adolescent girls trafficked;
for teenagers coerced into gang allegiance;
for women laboring for a violent husband;
for migrants sweating in our fields;
for sexual minorities who must hide from assault;
for those unjustly imprisoned;
for all who because of their caste are constrained to serve others.
O God, release from bondage all who are held captive,
that your image may shine forth freely in each human person.
Amen.

Hebrews

*By faith Abel . . . Noah . . . Abraham . . . Isaac . . . Jacob . . . Joseph . . .
Moses . . . Rahab . . . And what more should I say? . . . Since we are
surrounded by so great a cloud of witnesses, let us also lay aside
every weight and the sin that clings so closely, and let us run with
perseverance the race that is set before us, looking to Jesus the
pioneer and perfecter of our faith. Hebrews 11:4-32; 12:1-2*

THANKING GOD FOR SAINTS

For all your saints, O Christ, Alpha and Omega, I praise you: for Ambrose, J. S. Bach, Catherine of Siena, Dorothy Day, Egeria, Francis of Assisi, M. Grünewald, Hildegard of Bingen, Irenaeus, Julian of Norwich, M. Kempe, M. Luther, H. M. Muhlenberg, P. Nicolai, F. O'Connor, Perpetua, Quodvultdeus, Radegund, Seattle, W. Tyndale, Ursula, the Venerable Bede, C. Winkworth, F. Xavier, C. Yonge, and—one of my favorites—B. Ziegenbalg. I laud you for each one. Can you please take some of the Spirit that was on them and put it on me?

O Christ, a footnote: I say that any fifth-century Carthaginian bishop who wrote about the Easter Vigil and was named Quodvultdeus deserves to be remembered.

To this I say Amen.

James

Listen! The wages of the laborers who mowed your fields, which you kept back by fraud, cry out, and the cries of the harvesters have reached the ears of the Lord of hosts. James 5:4

INTERCEDING FOR MIGRANT FARMWORKERS

O God, Staff of life, for just a few dollars
I buy lettuce and celery, mushrooms and onions,
corn and grapes, asparagus and garlic,
strawberries and raspberries, a groaning board of food,
thanks to the efforts of families of migrant farmworkers—
the pittance we pay them more than their homeland can offer.
Now, O God, Food for the world, I pray for the migrant farmworkers.
Awaken our full stomachs to their hungers,
so that they receive fair wages, proper housing, affordable health care,
nourishing meals, employee benefits, legal protections,
and schooling for their children.
Grant that sooner rather than later
your horn of plenty will be shared in a feast of justice,
you the Bread and the Corn and the Rice of life for everyone.
May it be so.

1 Peter

*Like newborn infants, long for the pure, spiritual milk, so
that by it you may grow into salvation–if indeed you
have tasted that the Lord is good. 1 Peter 2:2-3*

THANKING GOD FOR THE WORD

The truth is, dearest God of tender loving care, that we are all infants,
requiring each day the vigilance of others
who feed, house, comfort, inspire, and love us.
I thank you for the gift of your Word,
which feeds us with mercy, houses us in the church,
    comforts us in sorrow,
inspires us toward justice,
    and loves us despite ourselves.
I taste and see that you are good.
Give to me, O God, the milk of your Word,
me still a vulnerable infant, you the perpetually Nursing Mother,
freely giving us of your body,
cradling us in everlasting arms.
Amen.

2 Peter

We have the prophetic message more fully confirmed. You will do well to be attentive to this as to a lamp shining in a dark place, until the day dawns and the morning star rises in your hearts. 2 Peter 1:19

THANKING GOD FOR THE EASTER VIGIL

O Pillar of Light that is Christ, going before us across each wilderness, I am so glad each Easter Eve that I do not live as did my grandmother in Lake Wobegon during the last century, with its stark worship practices, but that in your mercy you have placed me where the Fire Ceremony of the Resurrection is celebrated, where for many years of my life with high delight I have gathered with the faithful in a dark place to gaze at the shining flame of the paschal candle, that flickering fire that dispels the darkness of our hearts and minds, as all those beloved readings are proclaimed once again and we sing and sing and sing all those Alleluias to you, the Morning Star that never sets, beckoning us through each night toward your day. Amen.

1 John

*This is the message we proclaim to you, that God is
light. . . . The darkness is passing away and the
true light is already shining. 1 John 1:5; 2:8*

Praising God, Light and Darkness

O God, Plenitude of light, Center of the sun, and Fullness of darkness,
I praise you, God who is Light, without whom there is no life.
You ignited the shimmering stars before human time,
you shine on leaves so that the trees may thrive,
you send the dawn to rouse the children for school.
But I say to the ancient author:
I praise you, God who is also Darkness,
who will never pass away,
in whom is the sleep that our bodies require,
in whom we grope when there is no sight,
to whom we feel our way at the close of our days.
This is a comfort: God is Light, God is Darkness.
This God I praise.
Amen.

2 John

*The elder to the elect lady and her children, whom I love
in the truth . . . : I was overjoyed to find some of
your children walking in the truth. 2 John 1, 4*

Interceding for future generations

O God, the Foundation of a changing world,
the Cornerstone of our lives,
and Framework for the future,
I pray for our children, grandchildren, great-grandchildren:
may future generations keep the faith of Christ's resurrection,
honoring you,
striving to discern what is meant by this "truth,"
praying at meals,
assembling each Sunday,
sharing divine food,
standing with the saints to hand over the creed yet again,
serving the needy in the hope for justice.
Receive this prayer, O God, for the twenty-second century,
which will need religion as much as we do.
Amen.

3 John

Whoever does good is from God; whoever
does evil has not seen God. 3 John 11

Interceding for the nones

O God beyond religion, outside our logic, reordering our systems,
here your ancient author seems to approve the nones,
those who live honorably without any worship of you,
who avoid evil more consistently than many who are driven by belief.
So although I am a full-time advocate of worthy religions,
I pray for the nones,
for the increasing numbers of those
who quite without the support of any organized religion
do good for the world,
unaware that their good reflects you.
Give them, Great Spirit,
noble purpose, companions in goodness, and contagious joy,
and open my mind to their virtue.
May it be so.

Jude

Certain intruders have stolen in among you. Woe to them! For they go the way of Cain. They are wandering stars, for whom the deepest darkness has been reserved forever. Jude 4, 11, 13

Interceding for no hell

Beneficent Maker, Forgiver, and Restorer of all things, I am stunned by the vengeful rhetoric of this "Jude," who sounds delighted that at the end of time the fallen angels, unbelieving Israelites, residents of Sodom and Gomorrah, Cain, Balaam, Korah and his gang, the whole lot of them will be punished with your eternal fire forever.

Receive my prayer for those believers who fear intruders in their midst. Receive my prayer for those believers who relish the notion of the everlasting condemnation of those whom they view as ungodly. Receive my prayer for all believers who literalize such biblical passages. Receive my prayer for an end to human vindictiveness. Receive my prayer for divine justice that does not necessitate burning torment for others at the end of time.

Give us yourself, O God, a different kind of divine essence, a deity who restores the fallen, accompanies the immoral, calms the malcontents, replaces their bombast with kindness, a god whose mercy contravenes the brutality in human logic. Give us faith in your life that does not need a hell to make us happy.

May it be so.

Revelation

*On either side of the river is the tree of life with its twelve kinds
of fruit, producing its fruit each month; and the leaves of the
tree are for the healing of the nations. Revelation 22:2*

PRAISING GOD THE TREE OF LIFE

How, O sempervirent God, could there be such a tree,
either on earth or after the earth,
one tree growing on both sides of the river,
one tree producing apples and apricots, peaches and pears,
    plums and pomegranates, cherries and olives,
    bananas and figs, coconuts and dates,
one tree healing the nations with only the balm of its leaves?
It is you, O God. You are this Tree of Life.
Praises to you, Tree of Life,
thriving on both sides of every divide,
providing the earth's diversity of foods,
removing the ache from sorrows and sufferings,
granting more fertility than our needs might imagine—
a bloody cross becoming blossoming beauty—
a Tree beyond all trees.
Blessing and glory and wisdom and thanksgiving
    and honor and power and might
be to this Life Tree forever and ever.
Amen.

To Conclude

And when you have finished praying through the Bible, you might try praying through your life, as did Polycarp, bishop of Smyrna, martyred in 156 at the age of eighty-six. The report of his arrest states that, with the soldiers waiting to escort him to prison, he "requested that they might grant him an hour to pray undisturbed. . . . He was unable to stop for two hours, calling to mind all those who had ever come into contact with him, both important and insignificant, famous and obscure, and the entire catholic church, scattered throughout the world." Your prayer, like that of Polycarp's, will take some time.

O God, my Beginning and my Ending,
our Womb and Mate and Tomb,
I remember before you all who have ever come into contact with me:
each member of my cherished family,
all my relatives, all my beloved ones,
my childhood pals and my college roommates,
my teachers and pastors and editors,
my neighbors and physicians,
the women in my book club,
each friend, each colleague, scattered across the globe.
O God, our Dawn, our Day, our Darkness,
grant them grace while they live and peace at the last.
Amen.

Concordance

Praising God as . . .

Thanking God for . . .

INTERCEDING FOR . . .

Scripture Index

Scripture Index

Lightning Source UK Ltd.
Milton Keynes UK
UKHW051815050722
405422UK00004B/122

9 781506 484990